THIS DEVOTIONAL BELONGS TO:

_____

_____

This book is in loving memory of my dad, Sam. He loved God's word and he taught me to love it, too. There's no greater accomplishment in a man's life than to see his children walking in the truth. I'm so thankful my dad invested his time and dedicated his days to point us to Jesus. Love you, dad.

NOTE FROM THE AUTHOR

I'm so glad you picked up this book! To get the most out of it, you might find it beneficial to pick one night a week to sit down as a family and read your new verse along with the corresponding devotion or prayer. Your devotion will help make the connection between just hearing the words in the verse and actually understanding more of how they apply in daily life. Each week's verse will be on a tear out card in the back of the book. Place this card in a spot that you'll actually see it! Our family spends a lot of time in the car so we put our verse on the dashboard as a reminder to practice it together a few times a day. The goal each week is to have the new verse memorized by the time the next family devotion comes around. You can even start your time by reciting verses that you've already learned to keep them fresh!

My prayer is that your family grows in faith together and creates deep roots in God's word.

-Laura Godfrey

A gentle answer turns away wrath but a harsh word stirs up anger

Proverbs 15:1

VERSE

> *A gentle answer turns away wrath, but a harsh word stirs up anger.*

Proverbs 15:1

Wouldn't it be nice if we were gentle with each other all the time? It's a little easier to be gentle when someone is being gentle with you, but what about when someone is being harsh? When you hear an angry tone or feel that anger bubbling up in someone else, it's so easy to just fight anger with anger. This verse teaches us how to respond to unkindness, and it's always with gentleness. When we are gentle, it helps calm the anger. How amazing is that? What a wonderful way to help someone who is struggling with anger—by choosing to be gentle and helping to turn away the wrath that's probably making them feel yucky too. Next time you feel angry or face someone who is angry, remember that when you choose to be gentle, you're changing the course of the conversation, which is going to be good for you and for them!

TALK ABOUT IT

Can you think of a time when someone who could have been angry with you responded with gentleness instead?

Therefore, as God's chosen people, HOLY and dearly loved, clothe yourselves with compassion, kindness, HUMILITY, GENTLENESS and patience

Colossians 3:12

VERSE

> *Therefore, as God's chosen people, holy and dearly loved, clothe yourselves with compassion, kindness, humility, gentleness and patience.*

Colossians 3:12

Let's stop for a minute and just think about how amazing it is that not only are you one of God's chosen people, but because of what Jesus did on the cross, you are holy in Him, and because you belong to Him, you are also dearly loved. Think about what it means to be dearly loved by God. The Creator of all things. The One who holds all things together. Nothing happens without Him seeing it. No one is here without Him knowing it. He is unlimited in power and wisdom, and yet He loves you. He knows your name and your favorite color. He knows the number of hairs on your head, and He loves every one. Whenever you're tempted to think that you aren't valuable or important, just look around you at this beautiful world and remember that you were created, chosen, and dearly loved.

TALK ABOUT IT

Think about something you see in God's creation that reminds you of how much He loves you.

the Lord is
my strength
and my
shield

Psalm 28:7

VERSE

> *The Lord is my strength and my shield; my heart trusts in him, and he helps me. My heart leaps for joy, and with my song I will praise him.*

Psalm 28:7

I've always really enjoyed watching sports movies. When I was younger, some of my favorites were The Mighty Ducks, The Big Green, and Little Giants. I always enjoyed cheering for the underdog, but I especially loved the ending of the movie when the team overcame their obstacles and won the big game. Then there was the moment when the star player would leap into the air, their fist raised to the sky, and you could just taste the victory. That's exactly what I picture when I think of a heart leaping for joy. God is our strength and our victory, and because of the help He gives us, we can have our own slow-motion, end-of-the-movie victory jump to praise Him for all He has done for us.

TALK ABOUT IT

Do you have a favorite scene in a sports movie? What is something you've seen God do recently that made you want to jump for joy?

While we were still *sinners* Christ died for us!

Romans 5:8

VERSE

But God demonstrates his own love for us in this: While we were still sinners, Christ died for us.

Romans 5:8

 PRAY TOGETHER

Dear God, thank You for how much You love me. Thank You for not waiting until I was good enough to show me how much You love me. You died for me even when I didn't deserve it. You didn't tell me to find my own way to heaven; You became the way to heaven. Please help me to remember how much You love me and to tell other people how much You love them too.

FOR WE ARE HIS workmanship, created in Christ Jesus, for good works, which God prepared beforehand, that we should walk in them.

Ephesians 2:10

VERSE

> *For we are his workmanship, created in Christ Jesus for good works, which God prepared beforehand, that we should walk in them.*

Ephesians 2:10

You are God's creation, and you were made for a reason. God's been thinking about all the reasons why you're here long before you were even born! Your big purpose is to do good things for God—and lots of them. You can use any gifts God has given you to do good. Think about a beautiful flower. One purpose of a flower is the beauty it provides. Flowers also help give us oxygen to breathe. And once it's picked and given away, a flower may help someone smile when they're having a hard day.

Sometimes it's easy to feel small and insignificant in this great, big world, but the Creator of all things made you. Not only did He make you, but He loves you and He thinks about you. Take a moment to thank God for creating you, and ask Him to open your eyes to see the small and big ways that He will use your life to do good things.

TALK ABOUT IT

What are some unique qualities and characteristics God has given you?!

Trust in the Lord with all your heart: Lean not on your own understanding: In all your ways acknowledge Him and He will make your paths straight

Proverbs 3:5-6

VERSE

> *Trust in the Lord with all your heart and lean not on your own understanding; in all your ways acknowledge him, and he will make your paths straight.*

Proverbs 3:5–6

To trust someone means that you put your confidence in them, that you believe they will do what they say they will do. Sometimes, even when God has shown us over and over again that He will care for us, we still slip into the mode of trying to take care of ourselves. We start to lean on ourselves instead of leaning on God. I remember a time when I had a lot of very important decisions to make. I was so afraid of making the wrong choice, and instead of bringing my worries to God, I just became anxious and afraid. Finally, I realized I didn't need to carry such a heavy burden alone. I wrote down all the things that worried me on a piece of paper, and then I tore it up and placed the pieces in a shoe box. I put the top on the box and put it on the shelf. It was my way of saying that I was giving my worries to God and trusting that He would show me what to do. In that moment, God reminded me who was in charge. When we speak this verse, we are saying, "God, I trust you, not myself. You are in charge, and I am not." The good news is that when we let Him take the lead, He will make even the twistiest paths straight.

TALK ABOUT IT

Is there something worrying you that needs to be written down, torn up, and put on the shelf?

Because of the Lord's great love, we are not consumed. His compassions never fail, they are new every morning, great is your faithfulness.

Lamentations 3:22-23

VERSE

Because of the Lord's great love we are not consumed, for his compassions never fail. They are new every morning; great is your faithfulness.

Lamentations 3:22–23

PRAY TOGETHER

Jesus, please help me to remember how much You love me. Every time I see the sun come up on a new day, let it remind me that You are faithful, no matter what. Help me to remember that even when I fail, Your kindness doesn't fail. When I feel sad, disappointed, or discouraged, those things will never swallow me up because I am covered by Your love for me. Thank You for loving me!

amen

Bear with each other, and forgive WHATEVER grievances you may have against one another. FORGIVE as the Lord forgave you.

Colossians 3:13

VERSE

> *Bear with each other and forgive one another if any of you has a grievance against someone. Forgive as the Lord forgave you.*

Colossians 3:13

When you were little, imagine if you made a big, huge, stinky mess in your kitchen and totally forgot to clean it up. Then when your mom saw the mess, instead of getting mad at you, she just said, "Wow! Looks like you had a lot of fun in here. How about I help you get it cleaned up so we can get it done faster?" Whew! What a relief that would be. Now let's imagine that the next day, your little sister made a big, huge, stinky mess in your room while you were gone. Since your mom had just been so kind in forgiving you, now you can do the same for your sister and even offer to help her clean it up so she can get done faster.

To bear with each other means to be patient with each other as we make mistakes—and, boy oh boy, do we make a lot of them! That must be why God reminds us to be patient with each other like He's patient with us and to forgive each other like He's forgiven us.

TALK ABOUT IT

What is one way you could be more helpful around your house?

teach me
your way
Lord, that
I may rely
on your
faithfulness

Psalm 86:11

VERSE

Teach me your way, Lord, that I may rely on your faithfulness; give me an undivided heart, that I may fear your name.

Psalm 86:11

One of my very favorite simple prayers to pray is that God would give me an undivided heart. I want my whole heart to belong to God, even in the midst of all the distractions around me. Every moment of every day, our hearts are being pulled in so many different directions. We get divided and don't even realize it. God is so kind and gentle with us. He hears every prayer we pray, and because of His faithfulness, He continues to teach us to depend on Him. As we depend on Him, trust Him, and let Him teach us, our hearts will be more and more fully His.

TALK ABOUT IT

Where is a place in your house you could put this verse to be reminded of it every day?

Do not be
anxious
about anything
instead, pray
about everything

Philippians 4:6-7

 VERSE

> *Do not be anxious about anything, but in every situation, by prayer and petition, with thanksgiving, present your requests to God. And the peace of God, which transcends all understanding, will guard your hearts and your minds in Christ Jesus.*

Philippians 4:6–7

There was a time in my life many years ago when I felt so worried and anxious about so many different things that I could hardly eat. I had trouble sleeping, and when I was awake it felt like all I did was worry. My stomach was in knots, and my brain was fuzzy from all the thinking I was doing. This is not how God wants us to live. To be anxious and worried is the exact opposite of what God wants for us. He wants peace for us.

To be at peace means to be tranquil or quiet, and the best way to quiet our thoughts is to tell God about them. We ask Him for help, we tell Him why we feel afraid or worried, and then we trust Him to take care of us. He promises that when we bring our worries to Him, He will make a trade with us. We give Him our worries, and He gives us His peace. Great deal, right? Then it gets even better. The peace of God stands like a security guard at our hearts, making sure those worries don't come back in and take over. There will always be reasons to worry, but God will always be ready to give you His peace. Just ask for it!

TALK ABOUT IT

When was the last time you told God about something that was worrying you and asked for His help in calming your heart?

Always be joyful.

never stop praying.

1 THESSALONIANS 5:16

VERSE

Always be joyful. Never stop praying. Be thankful in all circumstances, for this is God's will for you who belong to Christ Jesus.

1 Thessalonians 5:16–18

Have you ever tried to bake something and realized when it was too late that you forgot one of the main ingredients? Once when I was baking muffins, I totally forgot to add the eggs and didn't even notice until the muffins were already baking. Needless to say, those muffins had to go straight into the trash. When following a recipe, you have to get all the ingredients right, or it won't turn out like you want it to.

God gives us a recipe for how to be joyful. The two main ingredients we need are prayer and thankfulness. Prayer is simply talking to God. Being thankful is telling God how grateful you are for what you have. It sounds really easy, but when you get busy, sometimes you forget to talk to God. Not to mention that when you see what other people have, it's easy to wish you had more instead of being thankful. When you feel like you get off track or start to feel unhappy, sit down and talk to God, tell Him all the things you're thankful for. His promise is that you'll be filled with joy when you do.

TALK ABOUT IT

Can you think of three things that you're really thankful for today?

Commit to the Lord whatever you do, and He will establish your plans

Proverbs 16:3

VERSE

> *Commit to the Lord whatever you do, and he will establish your plans.*

Proverbs 16:3

Committing your ways to the Lord is a fancy way of saying that you trust God with your plans and believe He will care for you. Think about a time when you were younger and went on a trip with your family. When you got in the car to leave, you were trusting that your parents had put gas in the car, found directions, and hopefully brought snacks! When you commit your ways to the Lord, you're choosing to trust Him to take care of you. His promise is that if you trust Him, He will establish your plans. To establish something simply means to make it firm or stable. When you trust God, you are believing that He will help you stand firm when things are going well for you and especially when they are not. God will use everything that has happened to you in the past and everything that will happen to you in the future for your good and for His glory. Your part is to commit to and trust Him; His part is to care for you. And no one cares for you better than your Father God.

TALK ABOUT IT

What's your favorite vacation you've ever been on?

But let all
who take
refuge in
you rejoice.

Psalm 5:11

VERSE

> *But let all who take refuge in you rejoice; let them sing joyful praises forever. Spread your protection over them, that all who love your name may be filled with joy.*

Psalm 5:11

When I was growing up, we had a tornado siren right in our backyard. Any time we heard it go off, no matter the time of day, we would all go down into the basement to "take refuge" from the storm. Being in the basement was just the protection we needed in case the winds raged out of control. God says He is our refuge and our protection. Just as the basement kept us safe during a tornado warning, God keeps us safe during the storms we face in our lives. The writer of this Psalm is so thankful for God being a refuge that it causes him to sing for joy. When you sit and think about how amazing it is to have the Creator of the universe be your protection, you might want to sing for joy too!

TALK ABOUT IT

Take a moment to thank God for some of the ways He protects you.

Cast all your anxiety on Him, because He cares for you.

1 Peter 5:7

VERSE

Cast all your anxiety on him because he cares for you.

1 Peter 5:7

PRAY TOGETHER

Dear God, thank You for holding the things that feel too heavy for me. Thank You for letting me come to You and give You anything that worries me, scares me, or makes me feel shaky inside. Thank You for caring for me and making a way for me to trade my worry for Your peace.

Kind words are like Honey

Proverbs 16:24

VERSE

> *Kind words are like honey—sweet to the soul and healthy for the body.*

Proverbs 16:24

What's the nicest compliment anyone has ever paid you? That may be a hard question to answer, because while we may think nice things about people all the time, we don't say those things out loud nearly enough. I love this verse because it tells us that saying a kind word to a person can be like a healing medicine. Those are some powerful words! There are ways to practice kind words everywhere. You can thank the person bringing your mail and tell them you hope they have a great day. You can compliment a stranger on their outfit. Be sure above all that you use your words to speak kindness to those who are closest to you, especially your family.

TALK ABOUT IT

Is there someone in your family that could really use a kind word? Next time you see them, have that compliment ready to go!

MAY THE GOD
of Hope fill
you WITH joy
and PEACE as
you trust
IN HIM
ROMANS 15:13

VERSE

> *May the God of hope fill you with all joy and peace as you trust in him, so that you may overflow with hope by the power of the Holy Spirit.*

Romans 15:13

God is the source of hope, joy, and peace, which also means that He has an unlimited supply of those things to share with us. God doesn't want us to have just a little bit of hope, a touch of joy, and barely enough peace to get by. He wants us to be filled so much that these gifts overflow out of us and into the world around us. When people who don't know Jesus can get a taste of who He is just by seeing how His hope, joy, and peace flow out of us, we know we are pointing the world to Him. Only the God of hope can fill us up and keep us filled to the brim and overflowing. You can pray this verse any time you begin to feel you're lacking in the hope, joy, and peace department. Then watch as the God of hope does what only He can do!

TALK ABOUT IT

How would you act differently if instead of having just a little hope, you were overflowing with it?

be strong
and take
heart all
you who hope
in the Lord

Psalm 31:24

VERSE

Be strong and take heart, all you who hope in the Lord.

Psalm 31:24

What does it mean to hope in the Lord? Well, to hope in something means to expect something with confidence. This verse tells us that when we put our hope in the Lord, we can have strong hearts that are confident that God will take care of us. During times when we feel afraid or worried, it's especially important to remind ourselves of these truths. When your mind says, "There's no hope, and my heart is afraid," you can fight back with this word: "I am strong in my heart because my hope is in the Lord!"

TALK ABOUT IT

Is there a fearful thought that keeps showing up in your mind over and over? Practice fighting back with this verse next time it shows up!

my grace is sufficient for you, for my power is made perfect in weakness

2 Corinthians 12:9

VERSE

> *But he said to me, "My grace is sufficient for you, for my power is made perfect in weakness." Therefore I will boast all the more gladly about my weaknesses, so that Christ's power may rest on me.*

2 Corinthians 12:9

It seems a little weird to brag about your weakness, doesn't it? Most of us try really hard to keep our flaws and failures hidden because we are afraid of what other people will say or think about us. If our goal is to appear strong and capable to others, we just might be depending on our own power. When we can be honest about our weakness, it gives us a chance to rest in God's grace and see His power come alive in us. When God's power rests on us, we give Him all the glory for everything we accomplish through Him. You don't have to be afraid of your weaknesses, and you don't have to hide them. When we are weak, He is strong, and His grace gives us all we need to walk through the good days and the hard days.

TALK ABOUT IT

Can you think of an area where you feel very weak? Take that to God, and ask Him to be your strength.

A truly wise person uses few words.

PROVERBS 17:27

VERSE

> *A truly wise person uses few words; a person with understanding is even-tempered.*

Proverbs 17:27

If a wise person uses few words, then it's safe to say that they are also very careful about the few words they choose to speak. Being guarded with the words that come out of your mouth will help you to be even-tempered, able to keep your emotions steady. You will probably save yourself from some heated arguments by using fewer words and thinking before you speak! Here are a few ways to practice being a wise person of few words: Instead of just making statements in a conversation, ask questions. Instead of just assuming you are right, try to learn from others or the situation. Listen without just thinking about what you plan to say next. You can practice this right now by asking a family member a question about themselves. Let them talk, and you just do your best to listen and learn about them.

TALK ABOUT IT

What did you learn about your family member by just listening to them?

Be joyful in hope, patient in affliction, faithful in prayer.

Romans 12:12

VERSE

Be joyful in hope, patient in affliction, faithful in prayer.

Romans 12:12

I love very clear directions, but I usually can only grasp a few steps at a time. One time when I was visiting a doctor's office I'd never been to before, I asked for directions to get to the bathroom. What I heard sounded something like, "Take a left out of here, then take the elevator to the third floor, then get off and take a right, then a left. Then the bathroom is right there." I nodded like I had gotten all of it, but as soon as I walked away, I thought "uh-oh." I knew there was no way I was finding that bathroom any time soon. Now if I was told something simple like, "Walk out this door and the bathroom is on the right," I could handle that! One of the things I love about this Bible verse is that it's a simple instruction that's easy to remember. God tells us to be joyful, hopeful, and patient when things are hard, and to pray all the time. That's some instruction even I can remember! When life feels complicated or even a little scary, break it down to the basics and just remember this verse as a guide to get you through.

TALK ABOUT IT

Do you find it is most challenging to be hopeful, patient in hard times, or faithful in prayer? Which area could use the most practice?

those who hope in the Lord will renew their strength

ISAIAH 40:31

VERSE

Those who hope in the Lord will renew their strength. They will soar on wings like eagles; they will run and not grow weary, they will walk and not be faint.

Isaiah 40:31

There are few things more majestic than a beautiful eagle soaring through the sky. Whenever I see one, it always captivates me, and I can't help but just stop and stare. For a large bird like an eagle, there's a big difference between soaring and flying, even though they may look similar from the ground. Flying requires a flapping of their wings, which takes up a lot of energy. But when they soar, they are allowing the wind to glide them through the air with very little effort. Soaring is a rest time that allows them to gain more strength to flap their wings and move in the direction they want to go. God tells us that when we depend on His strength, He will renew ours. Just like the eagle depends on the wind to allow it to soar through the sky without using up all its energy, we can depend on God to be our strength that never runs out.

TALK ABOUT IT

What's the most interesting plant or animal you've ever seen? Did it make you think of your Creator?

Be strong
and courageous.
Do not be
afraid, for
the Lord your
God is with
you.

Deuteronomy 31:6

VERSE

Be strong and courageous. Do not be afraid or terrified because of them, for the Lord your God goes with you; he will never leave you nor forsake you.

Deuteronomy 31:6

PRAY TOGETHER

Dear God, thank You for being with me wherever I go. Thank You for telling me that I don't have to be afraid because I can always trust in You. Please help me to remember whenever I feel afraid that You are in charge of everything and everyone. The whole earth is under Your command. Because of the courage and strength that You give, I don't ever have to worry. I will trust in You!

THE LORD
gives strength
TO HIS PEOPLE,
the Lord
BLESSES HIS
children
WITH PEACE
Psalm 29:11

VERSE

> *The Lord gives strength to his people; the Lord blesses his people with peace.*

Psalm 29:11

Some of the best Bible verses are the ones that remind us of truths that are easy to forget. For instance, when you find yourself busy with school, sports, friends, church, and all kinds of other activities, the last thing you feel is peaceful. You probably feel slap worn out. Is it possible to feel at peace even when life around you is chaos? Well, the verse doesn't say, "The Lord blesses His people with peace . . . so long as their lives are already at peace." The verse promises peace as our blessing from the Lord. If you find yourself feeling anxious (the opposite of peaceful), it could be time to go before the Lord and ask Him to help you feel His peace. His peace is not dependent on your circumstances; it's dependent on His character. So you can always depend on His peace to be with you wherever you go.

TALK ABOUT IT

Have you struggled to feel peaceful lately? It could be a good time to sit quietly before God and ask for His peace.

A generous person will prosper, whoever refreshes others will be refreshed

PROVERBS 11:25

VERSE

> *A generous person will prosper; whoever refreshes others will be refreshed.*

Proverbs 11:25

It's easy to get so focused on ourselves and what we want and need that we forget to be generous to others. But God loves it when we are generous! He even rewards our generosity with a promise: that He will prosper us. The verse then goes on to say when you refresh others, you too will be refreshed. To refresh someone simply means to restore or renew them. Imagine you're at a restaurant and the waiter sees your drink is just about empty, so they ask if they can refresh it for you. They fill it back up! That's exactly what God does for us, but it's also what we can do for each other. One of the ways God takes care of His people is through His people. You and I are like tools in God's hands, and when we are generous and willing to refresh or fill other people up, we are giving glory to God, and He will honor that!

TALK ABOUT IT

Can you think of one way you could refresh someone by being helpful to them?

Be kind to
each other
TENDERHEARTED
forgive one
another.
Ephesians 4:32

VERSE

> *Be kind to one another, tenderhearted, forgiving one another, as God in Christ forgave you.*

Ephesians 4:32

Can you think of a time when a friend really hurt your feelings? If the friend came back and apologized, was it hard for you to forgive them? Now, can you think of a time when you were the one who did something wrong? Was it a relief when your friend forgave you? God tells us that we need to be tenderhearted and compassionate to one another, which means being gracious to someone even if they don't deserve it. God set the ultimate example of forgiveness when He died on the cross to save us from all the things we have done and will do wrong. He forgave us so we can forgive others. Next time you find it difficult to forgive someone, just think about how much God has forgiven you.

TALK ABOUT IT

When was the last time someone showed you compassion when you felt like you didn't deserve it?

give careful thought to the paths for your feet and be steadfast in all your ways

PROVERBS 4:26

VERSE

> *Give careful thought to the paths for your feet and be steadfast in all your ways.*

Proverbs 4:26

Few things are more embarrassing than tripping and falling. Just last week I was walking through a parking lot, trying to respond to a message on my phone, and I didn't notice the concrete block right in front of me. I didn't fall all the way to the ground, but I was really close! I looked up, and my face turned as red as a tomato when I saw how many people were around when I tripped. If I had been paying attention and not looking at my phone, I would have probably noticed the hazardous parts of the parking lot. You could say that I wasn't giving careful thought to the paths of my feet. The book of Proverbs is the book of wise teaching in the Bible, and one of the wisest things we can do is be careful about where we go and what we do. Be wise about the paths of your feet, and always pay attention in parking lots!

TALK ABOUT IT

What are some things that can distract you from making wise choices?

When you pass through the deep waters I will be with you.

Isaiah 43:2

VERSE

> *When you pass through the waters, I will be with you; and when you pass through the rivers, they will not sweep over you. When you walk through the fire, you will not be burned; the flames will not set you ablaze.*

Isaiah 43:2

Most of us would probably rather not have to walk through fire or pass through rivers that could pull us under. God tells us in His word that we will go through hard times, but the hope we have is that He will always be with us during those hard times. God was with Moses and the Israelites when they crossed the Red Sea to escape the Egyptians (Exodus 14). And He was with the three brave men in the Old Testament who stood up for their faith (Daniel 3). They were punished by being thrown into a furnace of fire! Yikes! Amazingly enough, God protected them from those flames. Not only did they not burn up in the furnace, they walked away without a single scorch—and everyone got to see how powerful God was. Even as you walk through difficulties, always remember that God is with you and His promises are for you.

TALK ABOUT IT

God gives us hundreds of promises in His Word, but is there one in particular that you're really thankful for?

He is able
to do
infinitely
more than all
we could ask
or imagine

Ephesians 3:20

VERSE

Now all glory to God, who is able, through his mighty power at work within us, to accomplish infinitely more than we might ask or think.

Ephesians 3:20

PRAY TOGETHER

Dear God, our prayer for our family is that our roots would grow down deep into the soil of Your marvelous love, and that we would have the power to understand, as all Your people should, how wide, how long, how high, and how deep Your love really is. May we experience the love of Christ—even though it is so great we will never fully understand it. Then we will be filled with the fullness of life and power that comes from You. Now glory be to You, God, for by Your mighty power at work within us, You are able to accomplish infinitely more than we would dare to ask or imagine. May You be glorified in our family and in Christ Jesus forever and ever.

Above all else, guard your heart, for everything you do flows from it.

Proverbs 4:23

VERSE

> *Above all else, guard your heart, for everything you do flows from it.*

Proverbs 4:23

We've probably all heard the expression "follow your heart," but did you know that this is actually really bad advice? The Bible says that the heart is deceptive, which means it can trick us if we aren't careful. We might just follow our hearts right into some very bad decisions. So instead of following your heart, God tells us to guard it. To guard your heart means to watch over it and protect it. The places you go, the people you spend time with, the movies you watch, the music you listen to, and the decisions you make will all have an effect on your heart. Be careful that all of these things are good for your heart and not harmful. If you've asked Jesus into your heart, you have His Holy Spirit living inside of you, guiding you to know what's good for you and what's not. Sometimes that funny feeling in the pit of your stomach is God telling you to stay away from something. What's really cool is that He is guarding you as you guard your heart, and He is the best guard of all!

TALK ABOUT IT

What's a song that you listen to that really lifts you up and encourages your heart?

DELIGHT
yourself
IN THE
Lord & He Will
GIVE YOU THE
the desires
OF YOUR HEART

Psalm 37:4

VERSE

> *Delight yourself in the Lord, and he will give you the desires of your heart.*

Psalm 37:4

To delight in something means that you find great joy or satisfaction in it. What's something delightful to you? I find great delight in a warm chocolate chip cookie straight out of the oven. Or enjoying a cup of hot tea while watching the rain. It's funny to think we can find delight in our favorite foods and also delight in the Lord. Obviously, the joy and satisfaction we feel for our Savior is much deeper and more meaningful than how we feel about a cookie. But think about the process of enjoying that cookie, and maybe you'll understand this verse a little more. When you enjoy a warm cookie, you're also enjoying the satisfaction of having something your heart desires. When we enjoy our relationship with God, the deepest desires of our heart are met in Him. When you spend time with God and get to know Him more, you find even greater joy in Him. As you find greater joy in Him, your heart gets exactly what it wants and needs . . . to be close to God!

TALK ABOUT IT

Can you name one thing that brings you great joy? Once you think of it, take a moment to thank God for the delight He brings into your life.

the Lord
will guide
you
continually

Isaiah 58:11

 VERSE

The Lord will guide you continually, giving you water when you are dry and restoring your strength. You will be like a well-watered garden, like an ever-flowing spring.

Isaiah 58:11

God isn't just a friend walking along beside us; He's also our guide. What's the difference? A great guide will know all about the area you're walking through, they'll know what you need for your journey, and they'll make sure you get to your destination safely. This verse reminds us that some days we feel weak, but God's strength never fails. God knows what you need before you even ask Him, and because He is such a good Father, He loves to take care of those needs. Take a moment to think about something that God has provided for you, and thank Him for the way He loves you and takes care of you.

TALK ABOUT IT

Can you think of a time that God guided you through a hard situation?

Walk with the wise and become wise.

Proverbs 13:20

VERSE

> *Walk with the wise and become wise, for a companion of fools suffers harm.*

Proverbs 13:20

The book of Proverbs is full of verses that teach us how to make wise choices. One of the most important decisions we make in life is who we choose to be close friends with. It's important to remember that God wants us to be a light to other people, especially those who don't know Him. But the writer of Proverbs gives us this warning— that if we spend time with foolish people, we could very well become like them. On the other hand, if we spend our time with people who are wise, we will grow wiser too.

You can be a friend to anyone and everyone, and you should be kind and respectful to all the people around you. But be very careful about who you choose as inner circle friends—the friends whom you spend a lot of time with and the people who will have the biggest impact on you. Need some ideas on how to spot a wise friend? A wise friend is someone who tells the truth, is respectful to adults, follows the rules, and is encouraging with their words, just to name a few qualities. You can ask God to help you find close friends who love Him and who will be an encouragement to you. You can also ask God to help you be that kind of friend to others!

TALK ABOUT IT

Can you think of a wise friend you have right now? What qualities make them that way?

We wait in
hope for the
Lord. He is
our HELP and
our shield

PSALM 33:20

VERSE

> *We wait in hope for the Lord; he is our help and our shield. In him our hearts rejoice, for we trust in his holy name. May your unfailing love be with us, Lord, even as we put our hope in you.*

Psalm 33:20–22

When you ask God for something, there are three possible answers He could give: yes, no, and wait. "Wait" may be the hardest answer of all because it really doesn't feel like an answer. God tells us that while we wait, we can still rejoice, trust, and hope in Him. He promises to shield us from what could hurt us and help us with the things we struggle through. If you're waiting for an answer from God, remember that the answer He gives will always be for His glory and for your good.

TALK ABOUT IT

Was there a time recently when God gave you a yes, no, or wait answer?

When troubles of any kind come your way, consider it an opportunity for great joy.

James 1:2

VERSE

> *When troubles of any kind come your way, consider it an opportunity for great joy. For you know that when your faith is tested, your endurance has a chance to grow. So let it grow, for when your endurance is fully developed, you will be perfect and complete, needing nothing.*

James 1:2–4

Most of us could probably admit that when trouble comes our way, our first reaction is not to jump for joy. That's probably the last thing we want to do! Following Jesus often involves changing our perspective so we see things the way God sees things. From God's perspective, He sees trials, troubles, and even pain as ways for our faith to grow as our endurance grows along with it. To endure means to carry on even through hardships. Life is full of hardships, so we all have plenty of opportunities to be really good at enduring! We don't usually get to choose what we face, but we always get to choose how we respond to it. When we respond to the hard stuff with an attitude of joy, it's as if we are saying, "God, I trust You and Your plan for me. Even when things are hard, You are still good."

TALK ABOUT IT

Is there something that's troubling your heart right now that you need God to help you see as an opportunity for joy, growth, and endurance?

When you speak healing words, you offer others fruit from the tree of life

PROVERBS 15:4

VERSE

> *When you speak healing words, you offer others fruit from the tree of life. But unhealthy, negative words do nothing but crush their hopes.*

Proverbs 15:4

Can you think of a time when you were really, really sick? Do you remember what a difference it made when you finally got some medicine and started to feel better? It's amazing what healing feels like, especially when you know how bad it feels to be sick. The Bible says when you speak kind and uplifting words to others, it's like healing for them. The opposite is also true. When you speak unkind and negative words, it crushes people. There's so much power in the words we choose to say. Our words can either be a gift or a curse. This should encourage us to be careful about the words we say to ourselves and to others, and also to be especially quick to speak words that will lift others up.

TALK ABOUT IT

Can you try finding one person each day to gift a kind word to?

the Lord your
God is in
your midst,
a mighty one
who will save

zephaniah 3:17

VERSE

> *The Lord your God is in your midst, a mighty one who will save; he will rejoice over you with gladness; he will quiet you by his love; he will exult over you with loud singing.*

Zephaniah 3:17

The Lord is with you whenever you need Him. The Lord is mighty, powerful, and able to save you. Nothing is too big or too hard for Him. The Lord takes great delight in you, which means that He feels joy and gladness when He thinks of you. The Lord is able to quiet your soul like a mom singing a lullaby to her baby, and the Lord rejoices over you like a great, big dance party! Always remember that whatever you need, the Lord will provide. He made you, He loves you, and He knows what you need before you even do!

TALK ABOUT IT

What is something you do that makes you feel close to the Lord?

How great
is the
GOODNESS
you have
stored up
FOR those
who fear you.

PSALM 31:19

VERSE

> *How great is the goodness you have stored up for those who fear you. You lavish it on those who come to you for protection, blessing them before a watching world.*

Psalm 31:19

Can you finish the line to this song? "Jesus loves me, this I know ..." You probably knew it right away, didn't you? This is one of the first songs we may learn when we are little, and even though the message is simple, it's very important. Just like the sweet children's song we've all heard, this verse reminds us that God has so much goodness, He wants to lavish it on us. Not only does He want to pour out His love and goodness on us, but He wants the rest of the world to see it. When our lives show others how good God's love is, they will want to experience His goodness too. You may know the ways God has been good to you, but be sure to tell other people so that they know too!

TALK ABOUT IT

Can you think of two ways that God has shown His goodness to you?

rejoice
always
pray without
ceasing.

1 THESSALONIANS 5:17

VERSE

> *Rejoice always, pray without ceasing, give thanks in all circumstances; for this is the will of God in Christ Jesus for you.*

1 Thessalonians 5:16–18

One of the quickest ways to shift your perspective is to be thankful. Try this out: Instead of saying, "I have to," switch to, "I get to." If you would normally say, "I have to clean my room," try saying, "I get to clean my room," which makes it sound like you're glad to do it. Saying that you get to do something can help remind you of what you have to be thankful for. Having a room to clean means that you have special items strewn about on that floor of yours. You also have a comfortable bed you get to make and maybe even a bathroom with a toilet and running water that you get to clean. Giving thanks to God for what you have and what you get to do will lead to even more thankfulness. Having a thankful heart is part of God's will for your life!

TALK ABOUT IT

What are two things you GET to do every day? Share them and why you are thankful you get to do them!

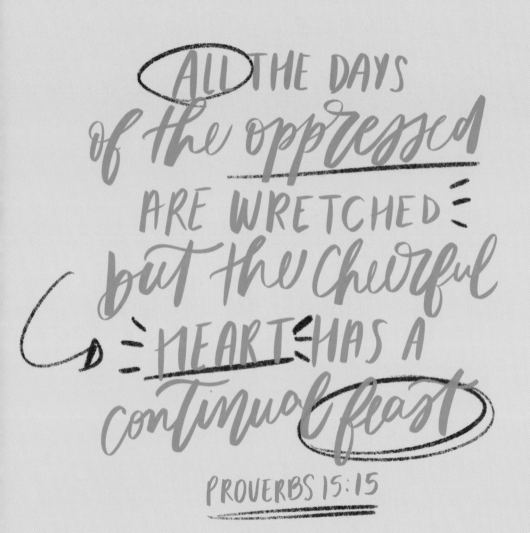

All the days of the oppressed are wretched but the cheerful heart has a continual feast

PROVERBS 15:15

VERSE

> *All the days of the oppressed are wretched, but the cheerful heart has a continual feast.*

Proverbs 15:15

Being cheerful is a choice. We get to decide how we respond to the things that happen to us, and the Bible says that when we choose to respond with a cheerful attitude, it's like a feast. When I think of a feast, I think of Thanksgiving dinner or a huge party, where all of my favorite foods and desserts are covering the table, and everyone is enjoying the food and company. But this verse is not talking about just any feast—this is a feast that never ends!

On the other hand, when we respond by feeling sorry for ourselves and having a negative attitude, our days will continue to be miserable. One of the most important things to remember is that God gives us the power to choose our attitude. It may seem really hard some days to choose a cheerful attitude. Especially on those days when everything seems to go wrong. Remember that bad moments don't make bad days. God can always turn things around, and you can ask Him for help when choosing to be cheerful.

TALK ABOUT IT

Have you ever had an opportunity to choose to be cheerful even when things were hard? How did your attitude change the way you saw your situation?

Dear friends, let us love one another for love comes from God.

1 John 4:7

VERSE

> *Dear friends, let us love one another, for love comes from God. Everyone who loves has been born of God and knows God. Whoever does not love does not know God, because God is love.*

1 John 4:7–8

Agape love is the kind of love that is selfless and unconditional. This kind of love doesn't say, "I will only love you when you are lovable." It says, "I will love you no matter what." God sets the perfect example of agape love in the way He loves us just as we are, even when we are unlovable. How we respond to this love really matters. Whenever it feels difficult to show love to someone, remember how much God loves you. As God's love fills you up, it will overflow into the people around you . . . the people who deserve your love, and the people who don't. It isn't our job to decide who to love; it's our job to love like God because we are His and He is love!

TALK ABOUT IT

Can you think of a time when you felt loved unconditionally?

show me
the right
path, O
Lord

PSALM 25:4

VERSE

Show me the right path, O Lord; point out the road for me to follow. Lead me by your truth and teach me, for you are the God who saves me. All day long I put my hope in you.

Psalm 25:4–5

 PRAY TOGETHER

This is my prayer, Lord: I want to know Your Word and to let it be my guide every day. Help me to understand the difference between lies and truth, and to always choose to walk in the truth. You saved me, so I know I can trust in You. You made me, so You know what is best for me. You are all-knowing, so I will look to You to be my teacher and to show me the way to go. Thank You for loving me so well!

 amen

never let
ugly or
hateful words
come from
your mouth
Ephesians 4:29

VERSE

> And never let ugly or hateful words come from your mouth, but instead let your words become beautiful gifts that encourage others; do this by speaking words of grace to help them.

Ephesians 4:29

Most of the time when we talk, we are really only thinking about what the words mean to us. If we could shift our focus to how our words benefit other people, our speech would start to sound a lot different. Instead of bursting out in anger when we get frustrated, we might take a few deep breaths and wait to speak until we are more calm. Instead of talking about someone behind their back in a way that could hurt their feelings, we might choose to say something kind about them even if they can't hear us. Helpful words will always build people up. Hurtful words will always tear them down. If you find that you have a hard time speaking words that lift others up, ask God to speak through you! He is always faithful to help.

TALK ABOUT IT

Can you think of an example of words that would encourage and build someone up?

All things work together for the good of those who love God.

Romans 8:28

VERSE

> *We know that God causes everything to work together for the good of those who love God and are called according to his purpose for them.*

Romans 8:28

It's much easier to believe that God is working for your good when everything is going well—when you're getting along with your siblings, your entire family is happy, everything is going well with school. But what about when things aren't going your way—when tempers rage, no one seems to be getting along, you feel like what's important to you is falling apart? Choosing to believe that God is working in us and through us even when things are hard means having faith in what we cannot see.

We may not see God at work, but we have faith that He is. This is especially true when what we see makes us feel afraid. We may fear that God isn't going to take care of us, but our faith in Him and His Word reminds us that He is still at work whether we see it or not. If you find yourself feeling like things aren't working out, remember that God is always at work, and it's always for His glory and for your good. Trust Him and His plan for you. Faith and fear can't exist in the same place, so when you choose to put your faith in God, you're telling fear to take a hike!

TALK ABOUT IT

Remind yourself of a time when you felt afraid but God protected you and everything worked out.

One's pride
will bring
him low,
but he who
is lowly in
spirit will
obtain honor

Proverbs 29:23

VERSE

> *One's pride will bring him low, but he who is lowly in spirit will obtain honor.*

Proverbs 29:23

It sounds a little sad to be lowly in spirit, but God isn't telling us to be sad in order to be honored! Another word for lowly is the word humble. To be humble isn't to think less of yourself; it's just thinking of yourself less. It's interesting that a prideful person is usually someone who's trying really hard to be honored, but they do so by self-promotion, arrogance, and greed. When that is the motive of the heart, instead of being honored, you'll be brought low. When you make it your focus to be humble in heart, submissive to God and to others, and not heavily focused on yourself, it may appear you're being brought down. This verse tells us that the opposite is true! When you humble yourself, God will honor you.

TALK ABOUT IT

Can you think of a character in a movie who acts prideful? What about a character in a movie who's humble? What differences do you see between the two characters?

If you need wisdom, ask our generous GOD, & HE WILL give it to you.

James 1:5

VERSE

> *If you need wisdom, ask our generous God, and he will give it to you. He will not rebuke you for asking.*

James 1:5

Who is the smartest person you know? Can you imagine what it would be like to have this person with you all day every day? Any time you had a question or needed help with a situation, you could just ask them and they'd be happy to help. Even the smartest person you know is limited in their understanding, but think about how amazing it is that the God of the universe, who is all-wise and all-knowing, is listening to you as you talk to Him. Not only is He listening, He is ready and willing to generously give you discernment, common sense, and insight any time, day or night. His supply is unlimited, so there's no situation too big for Him and no problem too hard for Him. When you need wisdom, just ask. He's ready to give you all the wisdom you need!

TALK ABOUT IT

Is there a situation that feels too big for you to understand? Take a few minutes to tell God about it, and ask for His help.

THOSE WHO LIVE
in the shelter
OF THE MOST
High will find
REST IN THE SHADOW
of the Almighty
Psalms 91:1

VERSE

> *Those who live in the shelter of the Most High will find rest in the shadow of the Almighty. This I declare about the Lord: He alone is my refuge, my place of safety; he is my God, and I trust in him.*

Psalm 91:1–2

It's just this simple: the closer you are to God, the more you will rest in him. The more you rest in God, the more you're able to trust His ways, be obedient to His voice, and walk in faith. This is why there are so many stories throughout the Bible of people praising God even in the midst of terrible circumstances. Think of the apostle Paul being imprisoned in a tiny, dark, dirty cell. Was he complaining and worried for himself and his future? No, he was busy telling the prison guards about Jesus and writing letters to encourage churches throughout the world. He lived in the shelter of the Most High. He trusted God even when he didn't fully understand God's plan. Try spending a few minutes each day just sitting in God's presence. The more time you spend with Him, the more your soul will learn to rest in Him.

TALK ABOUT IT

If you were a fellow prisoner with Paul, what is one way you would try to encourage the other prisoners around you?

Blessed is the man who trusts in the Lord

Jeremiah 17:7

VERSE

> *"Blessed is the one who trusts in the Lord, whose confidence is in him. They will be like a tree planted by the water that sends out its roots by the stream. It does not fear when heat comes; its leaves are always green. It has no worries in a year of drought and never fails to bear fruit."*

Jeremiah 17:7–8

Once I walked through a forest after a massive storm had passed. There were limbs down everywhere and some trees had been pulled completely out of the ground, but there were also some trees that were still firmly planted in their place even after all the wind and rain. So what was the difference between the trees that were uprooted by the storm and the ones that were unmoved? The root system. The deeper and wider that a tree's roots go down into the ground, the stronger the tree and the better its chances are of withstanding storms and droughts. It's not the size of the tree above the ground that makes the difference; it's what's happening below ground. The same is true for us. As we let our trust in the Lord grow, our hearts become more and more rooted and established in Him. We who put our trust in God are not walking in fear and anxiety because we know that, just like a tree with strong roots won't fear the storm when it comes, we don't have to fear either!

TALK ABOUT IT

What are some things you could do to let your heart trust in God more?

WATCH your
Words and
BE Careful
What you
say

PROVERBS 21:23

VERSE

Watch your words and be careful what you say, and you'll be surprised by how few troubles you'll have.

Proverbs 21:23

The book of Proverbs is full of words of wisdom that teach us how to live our lives in a way that honors God. There's a reason so many of the verses in this book revolve around our words. When we choose to be careful about what we allow to come out of our mouths, it can protect us from all kinds of trouble. Have you ever had a situation where you blurted something out and immediately regretted it? It's a terrible feeling! The best way to avoid that feeling altogether is to practice the discipline of being kind, and when you can't be kind, to be quiet.

TALK ABOUT IT

Has there ever been a time when you said something you wish you could have taken back? Was it hard to apologize and make things right afterward?

THIS IS LOVE:

not that we loved God, but that He loved us and sent His Son as an atoning SACRIFICE for our sins

1 John 4:10

VERSE

> *This is love: not that we loved God, but that he loved us and sent his Son as an atoning sacrifice for our sins.*

1 John 4:10

God loved you long before you ever knew Him. He created you and knit you together before you were born. He loved you so much that when your sin separated you from Him, He sent His only Son to atone for you. The word atone means to make something right that has been wronged. But since we can't make things right ourselves, God made things right on our behalf. This is a gift He gave us. All we must do to accept this gift is to admit that we can't make things right ourselves and we need Him to save us. This is the Good News of the gospel, and the whole Bible is built around this beautiful message of God's atoning sacrifice!

TALK ABOUT IT

Has there been a time when you admitted that your sin had separated you from God and you couldn't make things right on your own? You can accept the gift of God's salvation by asking for His forgiveness, choosing to turn away from your sin, and walking with Him!

May the Lord himself, the Lord of peace, pour into you His peace in every circumstance

2 THESSALONIANS 3:16

VERSE

Now, may the Lord himself, the Lord of peace, pour into you his peace in every circumstance and in every possible way. The Lord's tangible presence be with you all.

2 Thessalonians 3:16

PRAY TOGETHER

Dear God, we pray that in the deepest parts of our hearts, we would feel Your peace. We ask that when people walk into our home, they would sense Your peace. We ask that in every conversation we have with one another, Your peace would be in charge of the words that we speak and the responses that we give. In every situation we walk through, help us to sense Your presence, for we know that true peace comes only from You. We ask that right here and now You would pour Your peace on us, and we thank You for what a gift it is to know You and experience the peace You give.

SURELY your goodness and LOVE will follow ME ALL the days of my life.

Psalm 23:6

VERSE

> *Surely your goodness and love will follow me all the days of my life, and I will dwell in the house of the Lord forever.*

Psalm 23:6

Isn't it amazing that this verse does not say that God's goodness and love will follow us so long as we are being good and loving? What is so beautiful about God's love is that it is agape love, which means it is unconditional. When you are walking close to God, He loves you. When you run from Him, that love doesn't change. You don't have to earn this love. It's given to you as a gift. God's goodness and love will follow you all of your days. Not just some of them. All of them. There may come a day when you hear a voice in your mind telling you that God could never love you. That is a lie! You are a wonderful, beautiful child of God, and you are loved no matter what. Rest in that.

TALK ABOUT IT

Have you ever felt like you weren't really worthy of God's love? Next time you feel that way, say this verse out loud to defeat that lie with the truth.

He holds
SUCCESS IN
store for
the UPRIGHT

proverbs 2:7

> *He holds success in store for the upright, he is a shield to those whose walk is blameless.*

Proverbs 2:7

A shield was used in ancient battles as a mostly defensive weapon. Instead of being used to harm someone else, the shield was used to protect the person holding it. When flaming arrows, swords, and spears would fly across the battlefield, the warrior would hold up their shield to block them. In Ephesians 6:16, it says that we as believers in God should hold up our shield to put out the flaming arrows of the evil one. The verse even tells us exactly what kind of shield to hold up: the shield of faith. Remember that our faith is our belief and trust in God. So when we read that God "is a shield to those whose walk is blameless," we find that it is our faith in Him that is also our protection. As you fight the battles that come every day, hold up your shield of faith, trusting and believing that God wins in the end.

TALK ABOUT IT

Can you think of a time you felt under attack but then saw how your faith in God protected you?

ABOUT THE AUTHOR

I am married to my high school sweetheart, Matt, and we make one kind of baby: blonde hair, blue eyes, GIRL. We have three of them and one on the way. We think they're kind of the best. We eat a lot of mexican food. I drink a lot of iced coffee. I play dress up for a living and I LOVE to share sale alerts and home finds on my blog. I rarely decorate a room and leave it that way for long. I like to share tales from the motherhood and ANYTHING we feel like is working to make parenting a little more joyful. My greatest goal is to help equip moms and dads to teach their children to know and love God's word.

ABOUT THE ILLUSTRATOR

Isabela Schielke is the owner and artist behind Isabela Schielke Studio. Her mission is to be a reminder of God's faithfulness. It may be from looking at one of her beautiful art prints after a long day or one of her hand-lettered stickers on your tumbler in the morning. She loves to create and inspire in hopes that you get encouraged by her art to remember that God is still in control of every situation and that He is in every season.

Therefore, as God's chosen people, HOLY and dearly loved, clothe yourselves with compassion, kindness, HUMILITY, GENTLENESS and patience

Colossians 3:12

A gentle answer turns away wrath but a harsh word stirs up anger

Proverbs 15:1

While we were still sinners Christ died for us!

Romans 5:8

the Lord is my strength and my shield

Psalm 28:7

"A gentle answer turns away wrath, but a harsh word stirs up anger."

Proverbs 15:1

"Therefore, as God's chosen people, holy and dearly loved, clothe yourselves with compassion, kindness, humility, gentleness and patience."

Colossians 3:12

"But God demonstrates his own love for us in this: While we were still sinners, Christ died for us."

Romans 5:8

"The Lord is my strength and my shield; my heart trusts in him, and he helps me. My heart leaps for joy, and with my song I will praise him."

Psalm 28:7

Trust in the Lord with all your heart. Lean not on your own understanding. In all your ways acknowledge Him and He will make your paths straight

Proverbs 3:5-6

For we are His workmanship, created in Christ Jesus, for good works, which God prepared beforehand, that we should walk in them.

Ephesians 2:10

Bear with each other, and forgive whatever grievances you may have against one another. Forgive as the Lord forgave you.

Colossians 3:13

Because of the Lord's great love, we are not consumed. His compassions never fail, they are new every morning, great is your faithfulness.

Lamentations 3:22-23

"For we are his workmanship,
created in Christ Jesus for good
works, which God prepared
beforehand, that we should
walk in them."

Ephesians 2:10

"Trust in the Lord with all
your heart and lean not on your
own understanding; in all your
ways acknowledge him, and he
will make your paths straight."

Proverbs 3:5-6

"Because of the Lord's great
love we are not consumed, for
his compassions never fail.
They are new every morning;
great is your faithfulness."

Lamentations 3:22-23

"Bear with each other and
forgive one another if any of
you has a grievance against
someone. Forgive as the Lord
forgave you."

Colossians 3:13

Do not be
anxious
about anything
instead, pray
about everything
Philippians 4:6-7

teach me
your way
Lord, that
I may rely
on your
faithfulness
Psalm 86:11

Commit to
the Lord
whatever
you do, and
He will
establish
your plans
Proverbs 16:3

Always be
joyful,
never stop
praying.
1 THESSALONIANS 5:16

"Teach me your way, Lord, that I may rely on your faithfulness; give me an undivided heart, that I may fear your name."

Proverbs 86:11

"Do not be anxious about anything, but in every situation, by prayer and petition, with thanksgiving, present your requests to God. And the peace of God, which transcends all understanding, will guard your hearts and your minds in Christ Jesus."

Philippians 4:6-7

"Always be joyful. Never stop praying. Be thankful in all circumstances, for this is God's will for you who belong to Christ Jesus."

1 Thessalonians 5:16-18

"Commit to the Lord whatever you do, and he will establish your plans."

Proverbs 16:3

Cast all your anxiety on Him, because He cares for you.

1 Peter 5:7

but let all who take refuge in you rejoice.

Psalm 5:11

MAY THE GOD of HOPE fill you WITH joy and PEACE as you trust IN HIM

ROMANS 15:13

kind words are like HONEY.

Proverbs 16:24

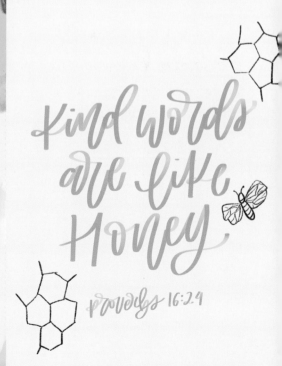

"But let all who take refuge in you rejoice; let them sing joyful praises forever. Spread your protection over them, that all who love your name may be filled with joy."

Psalm 5:11

"Cast all your anxiety on him because he cares for you."

1 Peter 5:7

"Kind words are like honey— sweet to the soul and healthy for the body."

Proverbs 16:24

"May the God of hope fill you with all joy and peace as you trust in him, so that you may overflow with hope by the power of the Holy Spirit."

Romans 15:13

my grace is
sufficient
for you, for
my power is
made perfect
in weakness

2 Corinthians 12:9

Be strong
and take
heart all
you who hope
in the Lord

Psalm 31:24

Be joyful in
hope, patient
in affliction,
faithful in
prayer.

Romans 12:12

A truly wise
person uses
few words.

PROVERBS 17:27

"Be strong and take heart, all you who hope in the Lord."

Psalm 31:24

"But he said to me, "My grace is sufficient for you, for my power is made perfect in weakness." Therefore I will boast all the more gladly about my weaknesses, so that Christ's power may rest on me."

1 Corinthians 12:9

"A truly wise person uses few words; a person with understanding is even-tempered."

Proverbs 17:27

"Be joyful in hope, patient in affliction, faithful in prayer."

Romans 12:12

Be strong
and courageous.
Do not be
afraid, for
the Lord your
God is with
you.

Deuteronomy 31:6

those who
hope in the
Lord will
renew their
strength

ISAIAH 40:31

A generous
person will
prosper, whoever
refreshes others
will be
refreshed

PROVERBS 11:25

THE LORD
gives strength
TO HIS PEOPLE,
the Lord
BLESSES HIS
Children
WITH PEACE

Psalm 29:11

"Those who hope in the Lord will renew their strength. They will soar on wings like eagles; they will run and not grow weary, they will walk and not be faint."

Isaiah 40:31

"Be strong and courageous. Do not be afraid or terrified because of them, for the Lord your God goes with you; he will never leave you nor forsake you."

Deuteronomy 31:6

"The Lord gives strength to his people; the Lord blesses his people with peace."

Psalm 29:11

"A generous person will prosper; whoever refreshes others will be refreshed."

Proverbs 11:25

give careful thought to the paths for your feet and be steadfast in all your ways

PROVERBS 4:26

Be kind to each other TENDERHEARTED forgive one another.

Ephesians 4:32

He is able to do infinitely more than all we could ask or imagine

Ephesians 3:20

When you pass through the deep waters I will be with you.

Isaiah 43:2

"Be kind to one another, tenderhearted, forgiving one another, as God in Christ forgave you."

———————————

Ephesians 4:32

———————————

"Give careful thought to the paths for your feet and be steadfast in all your ways."

———————————

Proverbs 4:26

———————————

"When you pass through the waters, I will be with you; and when you pass through the rivers, they will not sweep over you. When you walk through the fire, you will not be burned; the flames will not set you ablaze."

———————————

Isaiah 43:2

———————————

"Now all glory to God, who is able, through his mighty power at work within us, to accomplish infinitely more than we might ask or think."

———————————

Ephesians 3:20

———————————

DELIGHT *yourself* IN THE *Lord* & He will GIVE YOU THE *the desires* OF YOUR HEART

Psalm 37:4

Above all else, guard your heart, for everything you do flows from it.

Proverbs 4:23

Walk with the wise and become wise.

Proverbs 13:20

the Lord will guide you continually

Isaiah 58:11

"Above all else, guard your heart, for everything you do flows from it."

Proverbs 4:23

"Delight yourself in the Lord, and he will give you the desires of your heart."

Psalm 37:4

"The Lord will guide you continually, giving you water when you are dry and restoring your strength. You will be like a well-watered garden, like an ever-flowing spring."

Isaiah 58:11

"Walk with the wise and become wise, for a companion of fools suffers harm."

Proverbs 13:20

When troubles of any kind come your way, consider it an opportunity for great joy.

James 1:2

We wait in hope for the Lord. He is our HELP and our shield

PSALM 33:20

the Lord your God is in your midst, a mighty one who will save

Zephaniah 3:17

When you speak healing WORDS, you offer others fruit from the tree of life

PROVERBS 15:4

"We wait in hope for the Lord; he is our help and our shield. In him our hearts rejoice, for we trust in his holy name. May your unfailing love be with us, Lord, even as we put our hope in you."

Psalm 33:20-22

"When troubles of any kind come your way, consider it an opportunity for great joy. For you know that when your faith is tested, your endurance has a chance to grow. So let it grow, for when your endurance is fully developed, you will be perfect and complete, needing nothing."

James 1:2-4

"When you speak healing words, you offer others fruit from the tree of life. But unhealthy, negative words do nothing but crush their hopes."

Proverbs 15:4

"The Lord your God is in your midst, a mighty one who will save; he will rejoice over you with gladness; he will quiet you by his love; he will exult over you with loud singing."

Zephaniah 3:17

rejoice always pray without ceasing.

1 THESSALONIANS 5:17

How great is the GOODNESS you have stored up FOR those who fear you.

PSALM 31:19

Dear friends, let us love one another for love comes from God.

John 4:7

ALL THE DAYS of the oppressed ARE WRETCHED but the cheerful HEART HAS A continual feast

PROVERBS 15:15

"How great is the goodness you have stored up for those who fear you. You lavish it on those who come to you for protection, blessing them before a watching world."

Psalm 31:19

"Rejoice always, pray without ceasing, give thanks in all circumstances; for this is the will of God in Christ Jesus for you."

1 Thessalonians 5:16–18

"All the days of the oppressed are wretched, but the cheerful heart has a continual feast."

Proverbs 15:15

"Dear friends, let us love one another, for love comes from God. Everyone who loves has been born of God and knows God. Whoever does not love does not know God, because God is love."

1 John 4:7-8

never let
ugly or
hateful words
come from
your mouth

Ephesians 4:29

show me
the right
path, O
Lord

PSALM 25:4

one's pride
will bring
him low,
but he who
is lowly in
spirit will
obtain honor

Proverbs 29:23

All things
work together
for the good
of those who
love God.

Romans 8:28

"Show me the right path, O Lord; point out the road for me to follow. Lead me by your truth and teach me, for you are the God who saves me. All day long I put my hope in you."

Psalm 25:4-5

"And never let ugly or hateful words come from your mouth, but instead let your words become beautiful gifts that encourage others; do this by speaking words of grace to help them."

Ephesians 4:29

"We know that God causes everything to work together for the good of those who love God and are called according to his purpose for them."

Romans 8:28

"One's pride will bring him low, but he who is lowly in spirit will obtain honor."

Proverbs 29:23

THOSE WHO LIVE
in the shelter
OF THE MOST
High will find
REST IN THE SHADOW
of the Almighty

Psalms 91:1

IF you need
wisdom,
ask our
generous
GOD, & HE WILL
give it to
you.

James 1:5

Watch your
words and
BE Careful
what you
say

PROVERBS 21:23

Blessed is the
man who
trusts in
the Lord

Jeremiah 17:7

"If you need wisdom, ask our generous God, and he will give it to you. He will not rebuke you for asking."

James 1:5

"Those who live in the shelter of the Most High will find rest in the shadow of the Almighty. This I declare about the Lord: He alone is my refuge, my place of safety; he is my God, and I trust in him."

Psalm 91:1-2

"Blessed is the one who trusts in the Lord, whose confidence is in him. They will be like a tree planted by the water that sends out its roots by the stream. It does not fear when heat comes; its leaves are always green. It has no worries in a year of drought and never fails to bear fruit."

Jeremiah 17:7-8

"Watch your words and be careful what you say, and you'll be surprised by how few troubles you'll have."

Proverbs 21:23

May the Lord Himself, the Lord of peace, pour into you His peace in every circumstance

2 Thessalonians 3:16

THIS IS LOVE: not that we loved God, but that He loved us and sent His Son as an atoning SACRIFICE for our sins

1 John 4:10

He holds SUCCESS IN store for the UPRIGHT

Proverbs 2:7

SURELY your goodness and LOVE will follow ME ALL the days of my life.

Psalm 23:6

"This is love: not that we loved God, but that he loved us and sent his Son as an atoning sacrifice for our sins."

1 John 4:10

"Now, may the Lord himself, the Lord of peace, pour into you his peace in every circumstance and in every possible way. The Lord's tangible presence be with you all."

2 Thessalonians 3:16

"Surely your goodness and love will follow me all the days of my life, and I will dwell in the house of the Lord forever."

Psalm 23:6

"He holds success in store for the upright, he is a shield to those whose walk is blameless."

Proverbs 2:7